DEVELOPMENTALLY APPROPRIATE PRACTICE

IN

SCHOOL-AGE CHILD CARE PROGRAMS

second edition

An Initiative of Project Home Safe

A Program of the American Home Economics Association
Funded in Part by a Grant from Whirlpool Foundation

DEVELOPMENTALLY APPROPRIATE PRACTICE

IN

SCHOOL-AGE CHILD CARE PROGRAMS

second edition

by

Kay M. Albrecht and Margaret C. Plantz

Project Home Safe

1555 King Street
Alexandria, VA 22314
703/706-4600

A Program of the American Home Economics Association
Funded in Part by a Grant from Whirlpool Foundation

KENDALL/HUNT PUBLISHING COMPANY
2460 Kerper Boulevard P.O. Box 539 Dubuque, Iowa 52004-0539

Typesetting by Ann C. Walsh

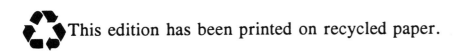 This edition has been printed on recycled paper.

Library of Congress Catalog Card Number: 93-077031

Library of Congress Cataloging-in-Publication Data

Albrecht, Kay M.
     Developmentally appropriate practice in school-age child care
programs / by Kay M. Albrecht and Margaret C. Plantz. -- 2nd ed.
          p. cm.
     "Project Home Safe ... a program of the American Home Economics
Association, co-sponsored by Whirlpool Foundation."
     Includes bibliographical references.
     ISBN 0-8403-8416-5
     1. School-age child care--United States. 2. Child development-
-United States. I. Plantz, Margaret C. II. Project Home Safe.
III. Title.
     HQ778.6.A43   1993
305.23'1--dc20   93-18006
                                               CIP

ISBN 0-8403-8416-5

Printed in the United States of America.
10 9 8 7 6 5 4 3 2 1

Contents

**Examples of Program Planning and Assessment
Tools Based on *Developmentally Appropriate Practice***

Appendices

Introduction

Project Home Safe is a national education and advocacy program addressing issues of child care for children ages 5 to 13. Begun in August, 1987, the project was conceptualized by home economists and is operated by the American Home Economics Association with a grant from Whirlpool Foundation, the philanthropic arm of Whirlpool Corporation. Project Home Safe promotes a range of community-based solutions to the problem of children at home alone. These include supervised programs that meet the developmental needs of school-age children and youth and respond flexibly to the work schedules and resources of their parents.

One component of Project Home Safe is an initiative to develop guidelines for quality programming in school-age child care. The initiative focuses on **child care** programs--programs that are accountable for school-agers' health, safety, recreation, and enrichment through a formal agreement with each child's or youth's parents or guardians.

Developmentally Appropriate Practice in School-Age Child Care Programs, which identifies principles and components of programming that reflect the characteristics and needs of school-age children, is one product of this initiative. A second document, *Quality Criteria for School-Age Child Care Programs*, specifies indicators of high quality in key program components.

Background

There is a substantial body of research on program characteristics that benefit children in early childhood programs--that is, programs for children from birth through age 8. In 1987 the National Association for the Education of Young Children (NAEYC), the nation's largest professional association for early childhood educators, published research-based statements of developmentally appropriate practice for programs serving children in this age range.[1]

There were no equivalent guidelines for child care programs designed specifically to serve **school-age** children. As part of its school-age child care quality initiative, Project Home Safe proposed to develop such guidelines with input from school-age child care experts and practitioners. Research on school-age child care programs from which to derive such guidelines is limited. Direction therefore had to be extrapolated from theoretical thinking, from developmental research on school-age children, and from practice.

The framework for this document resulted from a review of developmental theory and research literature which yielded key principles that should guide developmentally appropriate practice in school-age child care. NAEYC's developmentally appropriate practice statements were examined for concepts and issues pertinent to school-age child care programming. Those among NAEYC's practice statements that address the needs of school-age children and youth adequately were identified. Statements needing expansion or modification to focus specifically on school-age child care issues were highlighted, as were principles not addressed in the NAEYC publication.

In November, 1989, Project Home Safe sponsored a day-long working forum on school-age child care standards in conjunction with NAEYC's 1989 annual conference in Atlanta. Participants included representatives of Boys & Girls Clubs, Camp Fire Boys and Girls, National 4-H Council, the YMCA of the USA, the Wellesley College School-Age Child Care Project, the Center for Early Adolescence, the American Home Economics Association, the

---

[1] Bredekamp, S. (Ed.). (1987). *Developmentally appropriate practice in early childhood programs serving children from birth through age 8*. Washington, DC: National Association for the Education of Young Children.

U.S. Departments of the Army and Navy, seven statewide child care organizations, three state government agencies, and five state universities, as well as local program providers from 12 states (see Appendix 1).

These experts discussed key issues in school-age child care, including supporting positive self-concept and social experiences, developmentally appropriate supervision, experiential balance among activities, appropriate curriculum, parent-program relations, and accountability. Based on their experience and their knowledge of child care theory and school-age child development research, they described developmentally appropriate and inappropriate practices for various program components.

The practices identified by participants in the working forum were integrated into this document. The first draft of Project Home Safe's developmentally appropriate practice guidelines was reviewed by an advisory committee. The second draft was distributed for review by forum participants and other interested practitioners.

Developmentally Appropriate Practice in School-Age Child Care Programs

This document provides guidelines for developmentally appropriate school-age child care programming identified through the process just described. The first part of the document presents principles of developmentally appropriate programming with rationales derived from developmental theory and research. The second part illustrates the principles with specific practices--both appropriate and inappropriate--related to various program components. The third part--new in this edition--provides examples of program planning and assessment tools that can be created with this publication.

The first two sections of this document supplement the guidelines and practices for school-age children contained in Parts 1, 5, 6, and 7 of NAEYC's developmentally appropriate practice statements. Existing guidelines and practices from NAEYC's statements are not duplicated here. This document therefore should be used in conjunction with NAEYC's publication to enhance the ability of school-age child care providers to plan, implement, and evaluate developmentally appropriate school-age child care programs.[2]

School-age child care programs evidence the same range and diversity as early childhood programs. Just as NAEYC's developmentally appropriate practice statements aim to embrace this diversity while establishing broad parameters of appropriate practice, so this document seeks to identify components that transcend program philosophy or goals and to address the principal ingredients of appropriate programs for school-age children and youth, regardless of setting.

The rapid growth in school-age child care has created the need to articulate the field's best thinking at this time and make a first effort to identify the principles and practices of developmentally appropriate programming. This document is that beginning. As new research is reported, revisions undoubtedly will be needed. In the meantime, it is hoped that these guidelines can help those who plan programs for children and youth--including program administrators and staff, recreation specialists, school principals and teachers, and policy makers--design and implement programs that are developmentally appropriate for those who participate.

---

[2] For information about ordering NAEYC's publication, contact the National Association for the Education of Young Children, 1509 16th Street, NW, Washington, DC 20036-1426; 202/232-8777 or 800/424-2460.

Principles of Developmentally Appropriate Practice in School-Age Child Care Programs

Principles of Developmentally Appropriate Practice in School-Age Child Care Programs

The essential characteristic of developmentally appropriate programs is that their policies and practices are derived from the needs of the children they serve. This section of *Developmentally Appropriate Practice* identifies seven fundamental principles of developmentally appropriate programming for school-age children. The principles are based on the following standard.

> **Developmentally appropriate school-age child care programs are tailored to the developmental characteristics and needs of the children and youth they serve. Programs are mindful that children and youth change greatly during the school-age years and that the rate and nature of change vary considerably, both among children and youth and across developmental areas within the same child or youth. Programs approach these developmental realities as opportunities, rather than as problems.**

"Developmental appropriateness" has become common terminology to describe a specific orientation to programming in a wide variety of settings, both educational and recreational. Bredekamp (1987) identified two dimensions of developmental appropriateness: age appropriateness and individual appropriateness.

Age appropriateness refers to a program's congruence with the "universal, predictable sequences of growth and change that occur in children" (p. 2). For example, children achieve large-muscle coordination before they gain small-muscle coordination. Therefore, it is inappropriate to expect young children to master complex fine-motor tasks. Among school-agers, peers become increasingly important to social and emotional development. Thus, opportunities to interact with peers in a variety of situations are appropriate for this age group.

Children's development proceeds in stages. Each stage is distinct, characterized by abilities, attitudes, and priorities that are qualitatively different from those of preceding and subsequent stages. From kindergarten through junior high school, school-agers pass through three developmental stages. Specialists use various terms to identify these stages. In this document, the stages are designated as: *early childhood,* through which children pass between the ages of about 5 to 7 or 8; *middle childhood,* which characterizes children and youth from about age 8 to 10 or 11; and *early adolescence*, which extends from about age 11 to 14 or 15.

In school-age child care programs, age appropriateness actually means *stage appropriateness*: congruence with the characteristics and dynamics of these three stages. Differences among the stages and their implications for programming are discussed throughout this section on principles.

The second dimension of developmental appropriateness is *individual appropriateness*, which denotes responsiveness to each child's unique pattern and timing of growth. While development proceeds in predictable sequences through identifiable stages, different children progress through these sequences at different rates. Thus, two children of the same age often are at different developmental levels with regard to specific skills.

Further, children develop in several domains: physical, mental or cognitive, social, and emotional. Individual children mature at different rates in these different developmental areas. A child may be of average height for her age, for example, while showing more advanced cognitive skills and less social and emotional maturity than her peers.

During the school-age years, age becomes progressively weaker as a predictor of developmental level--and therefore as a guide to programming--because growth within developmental areas becomes more individualized. Sensitivity to the broader indicators of developmental stage and to the unique patterns of individual children and youth thus becomes increasingly important. Each of the following principles of developmentally appropriate practice for school-age child care programs is built upon the understanding that both stage appropriateness and individual appropriateness must guide adults who work with school-age children and youth.

> **Principle One**
>
> **Developmentally appropriate school-age child care programs provide resourceful, caring staff who understand the changing role adults play in school-agers' lives.**

As children and youth begin to look outside of the home for guidance and support, influential adults become sources of new information, new skills, new points of view, and different approaches to life's challenges and dilemmas. School-agers are fascinated by the things adults do and are curious and interested in figuring out more about adult roles and responsibilities. Adults serve as important behavior models and therefore can be effective coaches in encouraging prosocial behavior in children and youth (Oden & Asher, 1977).

Developmentally appropriate school-age child care programs use their understanding of these developmental characteristics to foster school-agers' development. They hire as staff people who have a repertoire of knowledge, skills, and abilities that are interesting and engaging to children and youth of this age. Thus, program participants see staff members as people who are resourceful and worth getting to know.

Staff structure their interactions with children and youth carefully. They see their primary role as facilitation rather than direction. Instead of instructing children and youth on what they are to do, they assist them with developing their own skills and abilities. Staff do this by setting the context, suggesting activities and experiences, providing guidance, and serving as resources.

Their facilitative role means that staff point out events that may be missed, offer suggestions, and provide encouragement and recognition for effort as well as recognition for accomplishment. It means that staff seek meaningful conversations with children and youth and spend more time listening to what they have to say than talking. They encourage school-agers to share experiences, ideas, and feelings and include them in conversations as they go about their work and play.

How staff carry out their facilitative role differs for children and youth in different developmental stages. Children in the early childhood stage (approximately age 5 to 7) can choose among a few options for activities but often have trouble generating options. For children in this stage, staff prepare the environment and provide suggestions for possible activities from which they can choose. They serve as motivators for participation in activities through their actions and their presence.

In contrast, children and youth in middle childhood (approximately age 8 to 10) are exercising increasing control over both their environment and their activities. Staff encourage children and youth to suggest activities and to assist in designing and implementing projects when appropriate. Staff also involve them in setting the stage (e.g., distributing materials, arranging props, getting out equipment). With early adolescents (approximately age 11 to 14), who are seeking greater autonomy and more adult-like roles, staff increasingly share responsibility for initiating and arranging activities, participating with them more as equals.

> **Principle Two**
>
> **Developmentally appropriate school-age child care programs recognize the increasing importance of peers to school-age children and youth.**

During the elementary school years, children and youth begin the developmental task of transferring some of their attachment from the home and the family to the larger world (Erickson, 1963). They begin to develop relationships with an ever-widening circle of friends close to their own age.

A school-ager's developmental stage with respect to social development is reflected clearly in relationships with peers. In the early childhood stage, peers are important as playmates because children are more interested in playing with others than in playing alone. However, relationships are situational. Children move in and out of groups based on their interest in the activity or experience, rather than on who else is in the group. Group composition therefore can be quite fluid (Selman, 1981; Shaffer, 1979).

As they move into middle childhood, children and youth begin to develop group relationships, affiliating with groups that help define who they are (Collins, 1984). The identification with the group inclines those in middle childhood toward same-sex and same-age groups. In early adolescence, youth begin to develop close individual relationships which can be quite enduring. Cross-sex interests also develop, compounding the challenge of negotiating peer relationships (Bergstrom, 1990; Maccoby, 1980).

Interactions with other children and youth provide the social context for school-agers to sort out what the world is like and how they fit into it (Bergstrom, 1990). Success in forming positive and productive relationships becomes the foundation for a sense of social competence that has lifelong implications. Research suggests that early difficulties in peer relations can have serious negative consequences for adjustment in later life, increasing the risk of, for example, delinquency, dropping out of school, mental health problems, and suicide (Asher & Coil, 1990; Asher, Renshaw, & Hymel, 1982).

It is important for staff of school-age child care programs to find ways to enhance peer relations and facilitate the development of social competence. This means creating plenty of opportunities for children and youth to participate in small, self-selected peer groups. It means planning activities that support and encourage emerging social skills such as initiating interactions with peers, maintaining relationships, and resolving interpersonal conflicts (Asher, Renshaw, & Hymel, 1982), making friends, affecting group outcomes, and taking on a wide variety of leadership and group participation roles.

Activities that help children and youth develop social competence with peers include role-playing social conflicts to explore various strategies and outcomes; reading and discussing books about friendship; negotiating program rules and consequences for misbehavior; working in groups to plan and implement plays, parent programs, and other events; discussing selections of new toys and materials for the program; and participating in special-interest clubs. Opportunities to practice social skills are broadened when staff use, and encourage school-agers' to use, different ways to divide into groups for activities: for example, by number of siblings, type of pet owned, or favorite recording artist, sport, or pizza topping.

Principle Three

In developmentally appropriate school-age child care programs, both mixed-age grouping and same-age grouping are used to facilitate the development of peer relations and social skills.

From the time they enter kindergarten, school-age children and youth spend much of their time stratified into same-age classroom groups. School-agers also benefit from interacting in mixed groups--particularly in groups where different developmental stages are represented. Mixed-stage groups may reduce competition between same-stage children, facilitate an understanding of the give and take in the real, mixed-age world (Bender, Schuyler-Haas Elder, & Flatter, 1984), and provide varying opportunities to practice prosocial behaviors.

Older children and youth in mixed-stage groups benefit from opportunities to exercise leadership skills (Stright & French, 1988) and to practice social skills with younger playmates who may be less threatening than same-stage peers (Katz, Evangelou, & Hartman, 1990). Younger children can get new ideas for the use of materials by observing older children and youth (Bender et al., 1984). Vygotsky (1978) contended that children's learning is facilitated when activities are coached by "experts." More capable peers, as well as supportive staff, can serve in the expert role.

Mixed-stage grouping is not appropriate when discrete skills and abilities are required for participation in an activity. Certain team sports, complex activities such as woodworking projects and science experiments, and certain social experiences such as cross-sex activities for early adolescents (e.g., dances, music) or discussions of age-related topics (grooming, puberty, health, etc.) work best in same-stage groups.

Children and youth also need to spend some time with same-stage peers who have similar interests and skills. These interactions help them learn participation in groups, increase their understanding of peer expectations and the culture of the peer group, experience social success, and enhance their social self-confidence.

Staff of developmentally appropriate school-age child care programs create opportunities for children and youth to interact in mixed-stage, as well as same-stage, groups. They offer many activities appropriate for mixed-stage groupings, including those in which older youth can help younger ones, such as board games with less-complex rules and strategies; drama, music, and dance; arts and crafts; snack preparation; team sports with minimal physical contact, such as baseball; and discussions of topics that are interest- rather than age-related.

Staff also identify school-agers of different developmental stages with a shared interest and involve them in a project related to that interest. They suggest mixed-stage activities to children and youth looking for a new undertaking. They predetermine teams for some activities to provide a mix of developmental stages.

The strategies staff use to encourage mixed-stage experiences are adapted to the developmental stage of the children and youth involved. Staff know that younger children have an innate interest in being with older children and youth, just as children and youth

---

are interested in being with adults. For children in the early childhood stage, the provision of high-interest activities generally is sufficient to encourage mixed-stage interactions.

For older children and youth, who may tend to associate only with same-age peers, staff create ways to meet other needs and interests within the context of mixed-stage activities. For example, staff pinpoint informal leaders among older school-agers and involve them in mixed-stage activities to encourage others to participate. Recognizing that children and youth are interested in interacting with adults, staff use themselves to attract older children and youth into groupings with younger children.

Staff also identify leadership and adult-like roles that older school-agers can assume in activities with younger children. They involve older children and youth as games librarians, equipment-inventory takers, or woodworking assistants. They identify program responsibilities that older school-agers can discharge, such as checking attendence, keeping snack containers filled, and picking books for the library center. They encourage older children and youth to plan and orchestrate a complex activity, such as a newsletter, a field trip, or an environmental project, in which younger children are involved.

When mixed-stage groupings are used, care is taken that older youth are not assigned roles as if they were extensions of the staff. They are not expected to monitor, nurture, feed, or otherwise carry out staff roles with respect to younger children. If such activities and relationships develop from the interactions between younger and older children and youth, they arise naturally rather than being imposed by staff.

Principle Four

Self-selection, rather than staff selection, of activities and experiences predominates in developmentally appropriate school-age child care programs. Schedules allow great flexibility for children and youth. Required participation in activities and experiences is limited.

The transition from early childhood to middle childhood is marked by a profound change in the way children seek, acquire, process, and evaluate information. In early childhood, children explore their world by observing and manipulating objects physically. Middle childhood, in contrast, is characterized by the ability to reason and think about things without having to experience them physically (Piaget, 1952). Traditionally, formal schooling builds on this ability by teaching children and youth a specified set of discrete skills related to reading, writing, and mathematics. These skills make children and youth increasingly able to examine and master the hows and whys of their world.

As their reasoning and learning skills grow, school-agers' curiosity explodes, as does their excitement about using their skills to explore whatever interests them. They are eager to pursue those interests and want opportunities to do so (Bergstrom, 1990). When the problems, activities, and questions they explore are self-selected, rather than assigned by adults, they are likely to probe longer and more thoroughly and to integrate new skills and knowledge into their developmental repertoire.

Because the traditional school day is fairly structured, with limited choices and required participation, it provides little chance for self-selected activities. Developmentally appropriate school-age child care programs give school-agers the opportunities they seek to apply skills acquired in school to pursuits of their own choosing. By creating ample opportunities for self-selection of activities, program staff expand participants' abilities to direct their own learning and enrichment. School-agers' need for variety helps ensure that they will pursue a wide range of interests and abilities.

In promoting self-selection, programs provide a balance to the school day by giving children and youth many experiences at the other end of the control-and-structure continuum. Initiative and effective decision-making skills also are fostered when school-agers are allowed to select their own activities.

To support self-selection, schedules are responsive to program participants' reactions to activities and experiences. This means that interesting activities are expanded and uninteresting ones are redesigned or shortened. Staff respect decisions by children and youth to participate or not, even when a child or youth chooses to do nothing.

Staff take on different roles with different developmental groups when providing opportunities for children and youth to direct their own activities. When working with children in early childhood, staff identify the activity options and help children evaluate those options and make decisions. They help school-agers in middle childhood add to the list of identified options and make choices from the expanded list. They assist early adolescents in devising their own list of options and negotiating both the list and the decision of what to do.

> **Principle Five**
>
> **Developmentally appropriate school-age child care programs use positive guidance and discipline techniques to help children and youth achieve self-control and develop their consciences.**

School-agers still are learning self-control. Although their temperaments are relatively stable, children and youth have strong emotions that surface in relationships with peers and adults. Children and youth benefit from adults who use positive approaches to help them behave constructively and solve interpersonal conflicts that arise.

A parallel task during the school-age years is the development of one's conscience through the internalization of society's rules and norms. Children and youth achieve this by learning about social expectations and by trying different ways of behaving and experiencing the consequences for themselves and others (Kohlberg, 1976). Adults facilitate this process by being positive social role models and by helping school-agers consider alternatives and evaluate outcomes (Curry & Johnson, 1990).

Staff of developmentally appropriate school-age child care programs use positive approaches to help children and youth learn to prevent unconstructive social conflicts. They structure and redirect school-agers' activities to prevent conflict from arising. They involve children and youth in establishing clear limits and rules that are tailored to fit school-agers' emerging skills. They explain reasons and rationales for rules as well as expectations for behavior so that children and youth can use this information in making choices about their actions (Marion, 1987). As school-agers mature, these explanations expand beyond the rules and expectations of the program to include those of society as well.

Staff also provide the context in which social problem-solving skills can mature with practice. They help children and youth evaluate different approaches to problem solving, see the natural and logical consequences of various behaviors, and practice negotiating acceptable outcomes to conflicts. Most important for school-agers' long-term well-being, staff help them see that conflicts and problems can be solved, often in more than one way.

Appropriate assistance with these developmental tasks requires different approaches for school-agers in different developmental stages. For children in early childhood, it means teaching discrete skills for appropriate social behavior, such as taking turns, dividing and sharing resources, and working cooperatively. Staff provide activities that help children practice these skills: board and card games, gross-motor games like tag and duck-duck-goose, and resources such as a woodworking bench that can be used by only one or two children at a time; making individual collages and construction projects with materials from a common pool; projects such as jigsaw puzzles, murals, and theme-based dramatic play (going to the pizza parlor or grocery store, working at the television station or airport). They also help children think about how their actions might make other children feel.

Assistance for those in early childhood also means managing the environment to avoid social conflicts that exceed young children's skills. For example, staff may delimit activity space to prevent more children from playing than there are materials. They guide children in presorting some materials--on trays, carpet squares, or placemats, in boxes, etc.--to encourage cooperative play. They provide duplicates of some popular toys and materials so that children do not have to wait to use them or get into custody fights.

For middle childhood children and youth, appropriate assistance in developing social problem-solving skills means helping them learn to enter and exit play groups, exercise planning skills, anticipate reactions, evaluate potential outcomes, and consider the consequences of their actions for others as well as for themselves. For example, staff create opportunities for children and youth to plan the daily schedule, allocate time to activities and projects, discover the outcomes of their plans, make modifications, and try the implementation again.

Staff provide other ways for those in middle childhood to experiment with different approaches to problem solving. They help children and youth list possible ways to achieve goals and choose among the possibilities. They encourage them to try more than one way to accomplish designated tasks without staff instruction about the best or easiest way. They promote role-playing or discussing possible solutions to social dilemmas. They assist with analyzing the outcomes of situations to determine what happened, discussing the result with understanding and non-threatening adults, and considering how consequences might have been different if alternative actions had been chosen in a given situation.

Social problem-solving skills of early adolescents are assisted by helping them learn to negotiate friendships in a group setting, experience the waxing and waning of friendships in a supportive environment, understand the appropriateness and inappropriateness of adult-like behaviors such as arguing or resisting authority, and practice taking on adult roles and behavior. Staff provide opportunities for early adolescents to learn the process of presenting opposing views while arguing with friends, practice separating emotions from points of view, and experience the consequences of resisting authority in a controlled and safe setting--losing privileges rather than being punished.

Staff also create ways for early adolescents to act "adult-like" with friends. For example, staff have them take on adult-like roles such as group leader, program planner, idea generator, or problem solver, or give them adult-like responsibilities, such as ordering food or trying out new recipes for snacks, purchasing games and materials, participating with younger children in activities, making and implementing plans for special events, and talking with potential staff members.

Principle Six

Environments in developmentally appropriate school-age child care programs are arranged to accommodate children and youth individually, in small groups, and in large groups, and to facilitate a wide variety of activities and experiences.

An important element of developmentally appropriate school-age child care programs is the environment that is created. What distinguishes school-age child care environments from traditional elementary school environments is the arrangement and individualization of the space. The physical layout and furnishings of the former contribute to developmental programming that provides for the varied ages, stages, interests, and needs of participating children and youth.

The environment is arranged to accommodate a variety of activities and experiences including individual, small-group, and large-group activities. Furniture is used to provide visual isolation of some areas, creating private spaces where children and youth can be alone and get away from the larger group. The varying abilities of program participants are taken into account in the use of space. For example, there are parallel activity areas (e.g., two woodworking centers) that require different skill levels and activity areas are equipped selectively (e.g., age- and interest-specific books in library areas).

The environment includes a sufficient variety and quantity of materials, readily accessible to children and youth, to meet their interests and needs. It has soft elements such as pillows, carpets, bean bag chairs, and gymnastics mats. Children and youth have many opportunities to personalize the environment with products of their work and play.

Providing a developmentally appropriate environment can be more difficult for school-age child care programs than for preschool programs because school-age child care often is housed in cafeterias, libraries, gymnasiums, or other facilities that are used primarily for another purpose. Restrictions on what programs may do with such shared space makes the creation of appropriate environments particularly challenging. Limited time to prepare space for the arrival of children and youth often compounds the problem.

Staff of developmentally appropriate school-age child care programs develop creative coping strategies for contending with limited flexibility of space. They use nesting storage systems that are set up and taken down easily. For example, games and materials are stored in cardboard boxes with the contents listed on the box top and the boxes are stored on audiovisual carts that are rolled into a storage closet. Art supplies are stored in individual containers (e.g., crayons in a shoe box, markers in orange juice cans, paper scraps in a shirt box, collage materials in margarine tubs) in a hinged storage unit that can be closed, locked, and rolled out of the way against the wall.

Program staff have access to the space in sufficient time to prepare the environment for school-agers' arrival. Staff also involve children and youth in setting up and taking down the toys, materials, and activity areas, making this type of activity a component of the program. In addition to helping with preparation of the space, this also helps children and youth personalize the space and supports their growing interest in assuming adult-like responsibilities.

> **Principle Seven**
>
> **Activities and experiences offered in developmentally appropriate school-age child care programs contribute to all aspects of a school-ager's development.**

During the school-age years, children and youth struggle to develop a sense of competence (Erickson, 1963). Competence--physical, cognitive, and social--comes from having many opportunities to practice emerging skills to the point of mastery and contributes to positive feelings about one's self. Staff in developmentally appropriate school-age child care programs provide activities and experiences that allow children and youth to feel industrious and to master new skills in all areas of development. They offer a wide range of activities and experiences to capture the interests of all program participants. They vary the pace and sequence of activities to provide balance among experiences and maintain children's and youth's interest.

> **Principle 7a**
>
> **Activities and experiences foster positive self-concept and a sense of independence.**

During the first 10 years of their lives, children and youth develop a complex set of concepts about themselves and begin to define themselves in terms of skills, preferences, and psychological traits (Maccoby, 1980). As these concepts develop, it is possible for children and youth to view themselves either favorably or unfavorably. Research has identified pervasive and significant differences in the social and experiential worlds of children and youth depending on the direction (positive or negative) of their view of self (Coopersmith, 1967; Gecas, 1982; Harter, 1986; Wylie, 1979).

A school-ager's self-concept, although not infinitely flexible or constantly changing, is sensitive to change (Webster & Sobieszek, 1974). Like most of his or her experiences, school-age child care has the potential to influence a young person's view of self. When staff offer children and youth plenty of opportunities to take charge of their own actions, affect the outcome of experiences and events, and direct their own activities, self-concept is likely to be enhanced. When the planned activities and experiences are not congruent with a school-ager's developmental needs--uninteresting, repetitive, too hard or easy, too restrictive--self-concept is likely to suffer.

In developmentally appropriate programs, children and youth have plenty of opportunities to experience success and accomplishment and to earn recognition for achievement from their peers and from caring staff. Children and youth also are allowed to place their own value on experiences, determining for themselves which experiences are important and which are not.

As competence grows, children and youth seek independence from the home and family. They seek to be in charge of their own activities and to escape adult supervision. Success with growing independence enhances both development toward adulthood and self-concept. However, school-age children and youth do not yet have all the skills and abilities needed to go unsupervised. They benefit from practice in situations where they can experience the responsibilities of independence within the confines of safety and with the support of caring and helpful adults.

Staff of developmentally appropriate programs support children's and youth's growing independence while recognizing the continued need for adult guidance. Staff encourage expression of independence by facilitating self-selection and initiation of activities, recognizing school-agers' preference for self-selected peer groups, offering opportunities to practice leadership skills, and creating ways to insure privacy. They provide preparation for new experiences, set clear guidelines and rules about behavior, and monitor children and youth as their ability to exercise independence grows. Staff allow program participants' involvement in planning and implementing the program's activities to increase as children and youth mature.

Principle 7b

Activities and experiences encourage children and youth to think, reason, question, and experiment.

Children and youth have a driving need to learn, although their methods of processing information vary with developmental stage. During most of early childhood, children need to touch or move objects physically in order to grasp concepts or understand relationships between objects. As they are leaving early childhood, they are developing the ability to manipulate objects mentally. During middle childhood, they no longer need to learn through physical manipulation and can think about and solve problems in their heads. Later, during adolescence, youth begin to acquire adult-like ability to think abstractly and comprehend systems of symbols (Piaget, 1952).

Children and youth in different developmental stages also evidence differences in learning styles and approaches to tasks. During early childhood, children tend to talk as they learn and to learn best when they are physically active during the learning process. The process of work often is more interesting than the resulting product, and children start many more projects than they finish. In middle childhood, as interest in the products of work increases, bringing projects to completion becomes important.

Realistic, adult-like activities become increasingly popular with early adolescents, who seek projects that result in real and usable products. The value of work takes on new meaning for them, and they exhibit more interest in long-term projects. They also want to take increasing responsibility for what they do and how they do it, using adult skills such as planning, implementing, and evaluating. Their approach to tasks varies, based on interest in the activity: if they are not interested, they will not participate.

The challenge of school-age child care is to provide an interesting and exciting context for children's and youth's need to learn. Staff of developmentally appropriate programs approach the cognitive aspect of programming from the perspective of enrichment, rather than acceleration, of learning. Staff understand that school-agers grasp new information and skills best when the concepts to be learned fall somewhere between their actual ability and their potential ability (Vygotsky, 1978).

This means that staff present children and youth with varied and interesting projects and tasks that encourage the elaboration of cognitive abilities without drill and practice. The subjects of intellectual pursuit are grounded in the contemporary culture and preferences of program participants. It also means that activities and experiences are neither too easy nor too difficult for the cognitive capabilities of participating children and youth.

> ### Principle 7c
>
> **Activities and experiences enhance physical development and cooperation and promote a healthy view of competition.**

School-age children and youth desire to be physically active and to increase their physical competence. When asked what they want to do, they often answer, "Go outside and play." After a long school day too often characterized by limited physical activity, many children and youth feel the need to go outside and exercise. Others seek restful, tactile experiences, such as sand and water play, clay sculpting, finger painting, and working in dirt or mud.

The mastery and application of physical skills is a major source of feelings of competence during the school-age years. Basic gross- and fine-motor skills still are emerging for younger school-agers. For older children and youth, these skills are in place, although coordination and control still may be uneven. School-agers are interested in perfecting activities that engage them and in applying newly mastered skills in a wide variety of situations.

Although their interest in physical activity is high, school-age children and youth need help planning and implementing physical activities and learning how to make group, team, and individual activities work. Making and understanding rules are arbitrary activities accompanied by a tremendous need for "fairness" (Lickona, 1983). During these years, children and youth play games with increasingly complex rules, sometimes replicating adult games with pre-set rules such as basketball, soccer, and football, and sometimes creating their own games and rules. They become competitive as they refine and practice physical skills and develop coordination and cognitive abilities.

Staff of developmentally appropriate school-age child care programs provide a wide variety of physical activities to insure that children and youth of all skill levels and interests have opportunities for physical exercise and practice to perfect both gross- and fine-motor skills. Large-muscle activities such as ball games, running, jumping, gymnastics, and tag enable children and youth to release physical energy. Both these recreations and small-muscle activities, such as board games, construction activities, woodworking, sewing, and a wide variety of arts and crafts projects, allow children to practice and perfect motor coordination and control.

Staff of developmentally appropriate programs consider school-agers' developmental stages in planning physical activities. Activities for younger children are non-competitive and promote practice of a limited set of skills. Fine-motor activities are simplified for this age group: they use thick pencils and crayons, cut out simple shapes, have blocks and puzzles with large pieces and simple connections, sew with large, blunt needles using long stitches. For those in middle childhood, staff plan both cooperative and competitive activities. They provide more advanced fine-motor activities and opportunities to coordinate a larger number of gross-motor movements, such as in basketball, soccer, and gymnastics. Staff offer early adolescents opportunities to use advanced skills, perfect their coordination, and practice coordinating their skills with the skills of others as a member of a team.

While school-agers are learning about making and following rules, staff often need to enforce established rules and facilitate discussions of fairness, as well as to help children and youth understand and learn about strategy. Staff work hard to help children and youth keep competition in perspective. They see to it that winning or losing is not the outcome of all group activities, routinely including games and projects that are cooperative rather than competitive in their activity plans.

When competition is included, it is not stressed. For example, children and youth have opportunities to play in tournaments where several games are played before a winner is declared; team composition is varied so program participants get experience with both sides of the win/lose equation; staff help children and youth keep track of game winners so they see that the occupant of the winner's seat changes over time.

Principle 7d

Activities and experiences encourage sound health, safety, and nutritional practices and the wise use of leisure time.

Children and youth form many preferences and habits during the early childhood and school-age years, including those related to personal hygiene, food, and personal safety. Also important during the school-age years is learning leisure activities--activities that prepare children and youth to reduce stress and in which children, youth, and adults participate just for fun (Collins, 1984).

By far the greatest contribution of school-age child care to children's physical growth and development is the establishment of a lifelong interest in and inclination toward physical fitness and physical activity. Concerns about school-agers' fitness that arise from sedentary lifestyles, eroding neighborhood safety, and long hours viewing television present a considerable challenge to the goal of instilling regular physical exercise as an important part of a balanced lifestyle (Collins, 1984).

Staff of developmentally appropriate school-age child care programs provide health, safety, and nutritional activities and experiences as a routine part of the program. They create opportunities to integrate health, safety, and nutritional information into daily habits, such as handwashing before preparing food or eating and after toileting. Staff provide children and youth with opportunities to talk with health practitioners, acquire self-care skills, take part in fitness activities, learn leisure sports, and participate in individual skill development activities.

Exposure to a wide range of leisure activities--including team and individual sports; recreational activities such as bowling, skating, or swimming; hobbies such as model building, sewing, or collecting; and craft activities that produce real and useful products--are all important for school-agers. School-age child care staff provide opportunities for such activities and encourage children and youth to pursue other leisure activities that interest them.

> **Principle 7e**
>
> **Activities and experiences encourage awareness of and involvement in the community at large.**

As children and youth make progress in transferring some of their attachment from the family to the larger world of friends and community, they need opportunities to connect with and participate in the world around them. In early childhood, children's exploration focuses on learning that they are members of the community at large. In middle childhood, becoming contributing members of the community and learning to function on one's own in the community are important tasks. Early adolescents are expanding their perspectives and experiences to include exposure to and exploration of the wider global community. Problem solving, consideration of societal issues, and appreciation for diversity become part of community awareness and involvement.

Staff of developmentally appropriate school-age child care programs create opportunities for children and youth to make these connections with the larger world. Beginning with the immediate setting, expanding into the neighborhood, and finally connecting with the larger community including the world of work, staff plan activities that help children experience the reciprocal relationship between themselves and the community and adopt a larger view of themselves in relationship to the rest of the world.

To explore the nature of the relationship between program participants and the community at large, staff encourage children and youth to read the local newspaper, invite resource people into the program, and arrange field trips to museums, work sites, cultural events, and community celebrations. They involve children and youth in community service projects and provide opportunities for participation in Camp Fire, 4-H, Future Homemakers of America, Junior Achievement, Scouts, and similar activities, and in local youth programs sponsored by fraternal and culturally based organizations.

Staff facilitate an understanding of diversity by treating school-agers of both sexes and all races, religions, family backgrounds, and cultures equally with respect, attention, and consideration. They help children and youth develop respect for diversity by making foods and apparel from various cultures, giving equal attention to religious and cultural events and holidays of all groups represented in the program, providing books and displaying pictures of a wide variety of cultures, and inviting parents and other visitors to share arts, crafts, music, dress, and stories of cultures they represent.

Staff seek to help younger children learn about some of their community's resources, such as museums, parks, and the zoo. They provide children and youth in middle childhood with opportunities to learn how goods and services used by their families are produced and delivered by others in their community and how they and their families affect and contribute to the community. They also help these children and youth learn skills such as making purchases and using public transportation.

Activities offered to early adolescents provide opportunities for becoming involved in discussing social, ecological, and other problems and for giving time and skills to address needs on an individual, community, or larger level. Examples include befriending the elderly, making audiotapes for children in preschool child care programs, and assisting in neighborhood recycling or clean-up efforts.

Project
HOME SAFE

A Program of the American Home Economics Association

Principles of Developmentally Appropriate Practice in School-Age Child Care Programs

Developmentally appropriate school-age child care programs are tailored to the developmental characteristics and needs of the children they serve. Programs are mindful that children and youth change greatly during the school-age years and that the rate and nature of change vary considerably, both among children and youth and across developmental areas within the same child or youth. Programs approach these developmental realities as opportunities, rather than as problems..

1. Developmentally appropriate school-age child care programs provide resourceful, caring staff who understand the changing role adults play in school-agers' lives.

2. Developmentally appropriate school-age child care programs recognize the increasing importance of peers to school-age children and youth.

3. In developmentally appropriate school-age child care programs, both mixed-age grouping and same-age grouping are used to facilitate the development of peer relations and social skills.

4. Self-selection, rather than staff selection, of activities and experiences predominates in developmentally appropriate school-age child care programs. Schedules allow great flexibility for children and youth. Required participation in activities and experiences is limited.

5. Developmentally appropriate school-age child care programs use positive guidance and discipline techniques to help children and youth achieve self-control and develop their consciences.

6. Environments in developmentally appropriate school-age child care programs are arranged to accommodate children and youth individually, in small groups, and in large groups, and to facilitate a wide variety of activities and experiences.

7. Activities and experiences offered in developmentally appropriate school-age child care programs contribute to all aspects of a school-ager's development.

    a. Activities and experiences foster positive self-concept and a sense of independence.

    b. Activities and experiences encourage children and youth to think, reason, question, and experiment.

    c. Activities and experiences enhance physical development and cooperation and promote a healthy view of competition.

    d. Activities and experiences encourage sound health, safety, and nutritional practices and the wise use of leisure time.

    e. Activities and experiences encourage awareness of and involvement in the community at large.

Examples of Developmentally Appropriate Practice in School-Age Child Care Programs

Examples of Developmentally Appropriate Practice in School-Age Child Care Programs

Program Component	Appropriate Practice	Inappropriate Practice
Staff Interactions with Children and Youth	Staff interact frequently with children and youth individually and in small groups as they work and play. They work in small groups on projects and participate with children and youth in games and activities, playing an active, integral role.	Staff interact predominantly with large groups.
	Interactions are reciprocal in nature. Staff seek meaningful interactions with each child or youth without dominating.	Most interactions take the form of verbal directions or instructions; there is little or no reciprocity of interactions. Staff interrupt children's and youth's activities, refuse to allow groups to define themselves, and interfere with individual autonomy.
	Staff seek meaningful conversations with children and youth, acknowledging their work, talking about events of importance, etc. Staff listen more than they talk.	Staff talk more than they listen. They respond similarly to all verbal interactions without taking the speaker's individual development or needs into account.
	Staff talk with individual children and youth and encourage them to refine and practice communication skills.	Verbal interactions between staff and children and youth are limited to directions and instructions. Little or no time is spent in informal or spontaneous conversations with children and youth.
	Staff speak to children and youth in low and calm voices. They go to children and youth to talk with them, rather than calling from a distance.	Staff use whistles, megaphones, loudspeakers, or yelling as the primary means to get school-agers' attention.
	Staff maintain a sense of humor as they implement planned activities. They take time to enjoy the spirit of the interactions and use humor to establish connections with children and youth. On-the-spot fun that emerges as children, youth, and staff work and play together is embraced and enjoyed.	Staff create a somber atmosphere. Humor that arises during interactions and activities is perceived as something to eliminate in case it might escalate out of control. Laughter by school-agers is discouraged.

Program Component	Appropriate Practice	Inappropriate Practice
Staff Interactions with Children and Youth (continued)	Staff respect school-agers' feelings and treat them with dignity.	Staff laugh at children's and youth's actions and behaviors or make fun of them when they work and play.
	Staff facilitate learning, social interaction, and involvement in activities rather than direct or instruct. They point out objects and circumstances that children and youth miss, help school-agers gain insight into their experiences, offer suggestions, and provide encouragement and recognition of effort as well as recognition of accomplishment.	The predominant role filled by staff is that of instructor and supervisor. Staff assume most or all leadership and supervision roles and attempt to guide all events. They see themselves as the only source of information and expertise.
	Staff treat children and youth of both sexes and all races, religions, family backgrounds, and cultures equally with respect, attention, and consideration and encourage the same behavior in children and youth.	Staff display differential treatment of children and youth based on gender or background. For example, participation in activities is based on gender stereotypes, such as "only boys play baseball" or "only girls cook;" children of blue-collar or ethnic-minority parents are steered toward physical rather than cognitive activities.
	Staff give equal attention to religious and cultural holidays and events of all religious and cultural groups represented in the program.	Holidays of some but not all religious and cultural groups represented among children and youth are observed, discussed, and/or incorporated into program activities.
	Staff understand the need for language-minority children and youth to have their native languages respected and accepted. They validate language-minority school-agers by learning words and phrases in the native languages of those enrolled. They give bi- or multilingual school-agers opportunities to use and practice their native languages and to share their languages with other school-agers in constructive and meaningful ways.	Staff give language-minority children and youth no opportunity to use their native languages. They meet attempts to do so with disapproval and demands to desist. Staff make no attempt to learn greetings or phrases in children's and youth's native languages. When school-agers are given opportunities to share their native languages, it is in superficial and perfunctory ways.

Program Component	Appropriate Practice	Inappropriate Practice
Staff Interactions with Children and Youth (continued)	Staff are in the physical or line-of-sight proximity of children and youth.	Staff observe children and youth from afar, getting involved with children and youth infrequently or only as problems arise.
	Staff position themselves strategically and are aware of the dynamics and activities of the entire group even when dealing with only a part of it.	Staff remain on the perimeter of the group. They are surprised when problems between children and youth erupt.
	Staff plan ahead to prevent problem situations from occurring. They use their knowledge of program participants' skills and abilities to anticipate where they need to be and what they need to do.	Staff intervention occurs most often after problems are present. Little is done to prevent the emergence of problems.
	Staff recognize the need of school-age children and youth for autonomy and independence.	Staff permit little or no unstructured time with friends.
	Supervision is based on the maturity of the child or youth, the type of activity, and the level of staff's supervision skills. Children and youth are given as much independence as is developmentally appropriate.	Supervision is predetermined and inflexible, not reflecting children's and youth's emerging independence or staff's supervision skills.
	Staff encourage independence in children and youth as they are ready. Opportunities to practice growing independence are an integral part of the program.	Staff see school-agers' emerging independence as a problem to manage and control. They fear that they will lose control if they allow children and youth to practice emerging independence and are unable to identify acceptable ways for them to do so. Staff discourage school-agers' attempts to learn and make decisions independently. They meet attempts to exert independence with stricter rules and less flexibility.

Program Component	Appropriate Practice	Inappropriate Practice
Activities/ Experiences	Available activities and experiences focus on all areas of development with consideration given to each program participant's total experience both in the school-age child care program and outside of it.	Experiences and activities are narrowly focused on one area of school-agers' development (e.g., cognitive, physical) without recognition that all areas of their development are interrelated.
	Activities are designed to enhance development and to allow children and youth to experience feelings of competence and completion.	Activities are either too easy or too difficult to capture school-agers' interest or attention.
	Staff take children and youth's emerging independence into account in planning activities and experiences. They recognize preferences for self-selected peer groups, create opportunities for children and youth to practice leadership skills, offer opportunities for earned recognition, and provide ways to insure privacy.	Activities and experiences ignore or thwart children's and youth's growing independence. Staff assign all activities and groups, discourage school-agers' input and discount suggestions or requests regarding activities and experiences, handle all decisions and arrangements at the staff level, and are intrusive in monitoring school-agers' activities and interactions.
	Experiences and activities are responsive to individual differences in abilities and interests. Each child or youth is viewed as a unique person with an individual pattern and timing of growth and development. Different levels of ability and development and different styles are expected, accepted, and used to design appropriate activities and experiences. Staff help school-agers accept and appreciate these differences in their peers and playmates.	Children and youth are evaluated only against a predetermined measure, such as a group norm or adult standard of behavior. All children and youth of the same age, regardless of interest or experience, are expected to behave the same way and perform the same tasks.
	Opportunities exist for individual, small-group, and large-group activities.	Large-group activities predominate.
	Children and youth play a central role in determining the activities and experiences in which they participate; choice predominates.	Staff determine the pace and sequence of the day and what activities will be available to whom.

Program Component	Appropriate Practice	Inappropriate Practice
Activities/ Experiences (continued)	Children and youth can choose not to participate in activities when they want to do so.	Staff misinterpret isolating behavior as indicating lack of maturity. Children and youth are required to participate when they do not want to do so.
	Visual media such as television, films, and videotapes are used as special events. The type and quality of media used is considered carefully. Information on audiovisual materials being used is shared with parents for their approval.	Television, films, and videotapes are used routinely to keep children and youth occupied and quiet. Parents are not informed about what materials are being used and cannot choose which materials their school-agers may and may not see.
Guidance of Social-Emotional Development	Staff encourage the development of social skills by arranging planned and spontaneous activities; allowing children to sit and talk with friends; focusing on the process of activities rather than the outcomes; encouraging children and youth to take responsibility for their own actions; providing opportunities for social recreation like tournaments, dances, trips, and interest clubs; and enabling children and youth to participate in committees that have real jobs and functions.	Social interaction and skill development are taken for granted as a byproduct of children and youth being in groups. Staff hope to manage interaction well enough to keep children and youth from being injured or hurt. No activities or experiences are planned to foster social skill development.
	Staff provide opportunities for children and youth to plan and practice their responses to social challenges.	Staff assume that telling children and youth what they should do is sufficient for them to use the behavior.
	Staff give children and youth opportunities to work out disagreements among themselves.	Staff are constantly on the alert to break up social interactions that might create conflict or crisis.

Program Component	Appropriate Practice	Inappropriate Practice
Guidance of Social-Emotional Development (continued)	Staff use positive approaches to help children and youth behave constructively. Staff describe problem situations to encourage program participants' evaluation of the problem; they listen and respond to children's and youth's evaluations. Staff help children and youth recognize the impact of their behavior on others by identifying feelings, facilitating social problem solving, and reflecting their expressions back to them.	Staff use techniques that hurt, frighten, or humiliate children and youth. They instruct children and youth on the solutions to problems rather than involving them in a discussion of the issue. The staff member's solution always is implemented, even when school-agers have other good ideas. Staff force children and youth to explain their behavior and make them apologize for misbehavior without discussing the cause or other circumstances surrounding the incident.
	Staff promote the development of school-agers' consciences and self-control through positive guidance techniques, such as setting clear limits in a positive manner, involving children and youth in establishing rules for social living and dealing with misbehavior, redirecting children and youth to an acceptable activity from an unacceptable one, and meeting with individual children and youth who are having problems.	Staff impose rules and solutions without input from children and youth. A single consequence, such as time out, is used for every misbehavior. Little attention is given to teaching children and youth more acceptable ways to achieve their goals.
	Logical and natural consequences and negotiated outcomes are used to resolve conflicts and problems.	Staff seldom include children and youth in problem solution. Consequences are primarily adult determined.
	Rationales and reasons for rules and expected behavior are shared with children and youth.	Expected behavior and reasons for rules are not explained to children and youth. Staff expect children and youth to comply with requests without having explanations of why they should do so.
	Staff maintain their perspective about misbehavior. They recognize that every infraction does not warrant attention and identify those that can be used as learning opportunities.	Staff react to every transgression. Their objective is to extinguish undesired behavior rather than to help children and youth develop social understanding and self-control.

Program Component	Appropriate Practice	Inappropriate Practice
Guidance of Social-Emotional Development (continued)	Foul language or cursing gets a response similar to other inappropriate behaviors. Experimentation with cursing is ignored when it occurs in isolation from other children and youth. Otherwise, it is redirected into appropriate avenues of verbal interaction. Group rules regarding foul language are developed in conjunction with children and youth and are discussed when foul language is used; logical and natural consequences are applied.	Foul language is treated differently from and more severely than other inappropriate behaviors. Children and youth who use foul language are humiliated, frightened, threatened with expulsion, or otherwise treated inappropriately.
	Staff intervene quickly when school-agers' responses to each other become physical. The inappropriateness of such responses and alternative solutions are discussed.	Aggressive behavior is met with aggressive behavior by staff who do not seek to solve the problem underlying the loss of control.
Enhancement of Physical Development	Wide variations in skill levels are expected and accepted. Activities that challenge more than one skill level are available routinely.	Only competent children and youth get to participate in some activities.
	Gross- and fine-motor activities are varied and interesting. Options for physical exercise include a variety of individual and team sports; exposure to different gross- and fine-motor equipment, such as balls and board games; construction activities; climbing equipment; time for running and playing; competitive and cooperative games; fitness activities; etc.	All motor activities are similar. Activities focus on competitive games.
	Restful fine-motor activities such as sand play, water play, play dough, modeling clay, finger painting, and digging are available.	Children and youth are given little opportunity to choose restful fine-motor alternatives to gross-motor activities.
	Craft activities take school-agers' different levels of skill into account.	Craft activities are limited in number and/or have no flexibility regarding components or steps, so that activities are either above or below the abilities of many children and youth in the program.

Program Component	Appropriate Practice	Inappropriate Practice
Enhancement of Physical Development (continued)	Staff plan both cooperative and competitive activities.	Competition is stressed in physical activities and winning is the primary focus.
	Staff encourage children and youth to use a variety of techniques to select team members for competitive games. They offer a variety of games requiring different skills and varying levels of complexity.	Little or no staff intervention is made in provision of competitive physical activities. Children and youth are allowed to choose their own activities and teams all of the time. No effort is made to vary the types of games played or to offset the developmental advantage that older school-agers have over younger ones.
	When competitive activities are offered, all interested children and youth are encouraged to participate, regardless of skill level. Staff help children and youth understand and learn game rules and regulations and learn about and understand strategy. They help school-agers negotiate rule modifications to fit different situations. They facilitate discussions of fairness when issues of rules and rights arise.	Children and youth are expected to know and understand the rules and regulations of competitive physical activities. Staff make no effort to help school-agers learn game rules or negotiate modified rules to fit different situations.
	Staff work hard to help children and youth keep competition in perspective. They help school-agers keep track of game winners so they see that the occupant of the winner's seat changes over time.	Staff dispense privileges based on winning; have ongoing competitions so there are winners and losers for the month or the year; or focus attention on a few winners through bulletin boards, parent newsletters, awards at family nights, or other means. The same few physically competent children and youth receive repeated recognition while others receive none.
Encouragement of Aesthetic Development	Children and youth have regular and varied opportunities for creative expression and appreciation through music, art, and dance. A variety of art media are available frequently for creative expression.	Aesthetic development is limited to art and craft projects which are available infrequently.

Program Component	Appropriate Practice	Inappropriate Practice
Encouragement of Aesthetic Development (continued)	School-agers have opportunities to write, produce, and present programs that are truly products of their own creative expression.	Staff orchestrate programs and determine which children and youth play what roles in the production.
	Children and youth have experiences that encourage awareness of and involvement in the community at large. Staff plan community service projects and arrange for school-agers to attend community events.	All activities and experiences focus on the children and youth themselves. No effort is made to help them recognize and understand their relationship with the larger community or participate in its life. Children are restricted to the program site.
	Creative art activities have no prescribed models; children and youth are allowed to create their own art. Art activities allow for school-agers' interest in products that have "real" function.	Adult-made models guide children and youth to complete art projects that all look alike. Displays of school-agers' work consist of multiple like products such as dinosaurs or butterflies cut from the same pattern. Little or no encouragement is given to experimentation with creative art materials.
	Children and youth determine what they do with the products of their creative work.	Staff determine the value of school-agers' work either directly by comments or recognition or indirectly by not responding to creative products.
	Music and dance are part of the aesthetic component of the program. School-agers' interest in contemporary music and dance is acknowledged and incorporated.	Music and dance are special events rather than an integral part of program implementation. Contemporary music is not accepted, recognized, or allowed.
Involvement in the Community	Children and youth have experiences that encourage awareness of and involvement in the community at large. Staff plan community service projects and arrange for school-agers to attend community events.	All activities and experiences focus on the children and youth themselves. Staff make no effort to help them recognize and understand their relationship with the larger community or participate in its life. Children are restricted to the program site.

Program Component	Appropriate Practice	Inappropriate Practice
Involvement in the Community (continued)	Staff arrange field trips into the surrounding neighborhood and community as one way of helping children and youth become involved in and aware of the community at large. Trips are diverse in nature. They are planned to help children and youth learn about community resources; understand the relationship between their families and goods and services produced in the community; and acquire skills for participating in the larger world. They also offer opportunities for school-agers to gain experiences in addressing community problems.	Trips from the program site are always recreational and are structured so that the children and youth take over a park, recreational facility, or sports arena. Integration of school-agers into the neighborhood and community is not a goal of leaving the school-age child care site.
Scheduling	The schedule has blocks of time for self-selected activities.	All activities are scheduled by staff.
	Activities that children and youth find interesting are expanded; uninteresting activities are redesigned or shortened.	The schedule is fragmented or inflexible and is directed or modified only by staff.
	The schedule provides appropriate mixing of indoor and outdoor activities, quiet and active play, small-group and large-group games, etc.	Certain types of activities predominate. For example, one day each week is designated for outdoor play; several fine-motor activities are scheduled back to back.
Group Composition	Group composition is varied and is determined by school-agers' self-selection among peers. Opportunities are available for older children and youth to help younger children and youth.	Staff determine grouping; little or no choices for group composition are given to children and youth.
Homework Support	Opportunities to complete homework are made available. Peer or adult tutorial help is available to children and youth who need or request help.	All children and youth are required to do homework. Homework must be completed prior to participation in other activities. Children and youth are expected to figure out homework assignments on their own.

Program Component	Appropriate Practice	Inappropriate Practice
Homework Support (continued)	Parents are viewed as school-agers' primary educators. Staff in school-age child care programs work with parents to coordinate homework completion.	Requirements for homework completion are determined without input from parents.
Parent Involvement	Information about children's and youth's needs and interests is obtained from parents during the enrollment process, is shared with appropriate staff members, and is updated regularly.	Staff view parents' input about their child or youth as irrelevant and make no effort to gather, record, or remember such information from parents.
	Parents are provided with information about program policies and procedures, including discipline philosophy and policies regarding termination of participation.	Parents find out about policies regarding discipline and termination of participation only after their child or youth has been disciplined or is being terminated from the program.
	Program staff gain understanding of each program participant's school, home, and other experiences outside the program and work in partnership with parents toward common goals for each child or youth.	Communication between parents and program staff focuses on giving parents information about the program and not on getting input and information from parents.
	Communication with parents is open and fluid. Information on a program participant's accomplishments is shared with parents as often as are concerns about the child or youth. Frequent and varied strategies are used to keep parents informed.	Communication with parents occurs on a pre-set schedule, such as once a year, and addresses specific topics. Communication focuses on the school-ager's misbehavior or problems in the program.
	Staff speak respectfully of parents and believe parents act in their school-ager's best interest.	Staff talk about parents in a negative way to other staff members and in front of children and youth. When problems arise, staff assume the problems arise from poor parenting.
	The program offers parents a variety of ways to be involved that provide all parents with real opportunities to participate.	Participation options are limited to parents coming to the program to meet with the staff or to participate in activities. All participation options require attendance at the program's site during traditional work hours.

Program Component	Appropriate Practice	Inappropriate Practice
Parent Involvement (continued)	Parents' satisfaction with the program is considered in program planning.	Parents are not asked or encouraged to provide feedback about their satisfaction with their school-agers' experiences in the program.
Staff Qualifications	Staff who develop and direct the program and staff who are directly responsible for children and youth have training and experience related to the ages of children and youth enrolled.	Staff are selected without consideration for educational preparation or experience. Staff have training and experience only in early childhood education or with school-age children only in academic settings.
	Staff are oriented to the program and participate in ongoing professional development opportunities.	Little or no orientation or pre-service training occurs before assignment to working with children and youth. Inservice training is not provided.
Administration	Site staff have access to program supervisors on a regular basis to discuss program issues, plan program activities, evaluate program effectiveness, and receive assistance with problem-solving.	Little or no supervision or direction is available to program staff--particularly staff at remote sites. Staff are required to make do without consultation from supervisory staff.
Group Size and Staffing	Group size and the ratio of staff to children and youth are limited to insure active involvement of staff and support for children and youth.	Large numbers of children and youth have few staff for guidance and support. Very large group sizes are allowed.
	Activity group sizes and ratios of staff to children and youth vary depending on the activity. For most activities, group sizes are no larger than 26 with two staff.	Group sizes of 20 or larger with one staff member are considered acceptable.
	Substitutes are available when regular staff are absent.	Both children and youth and the remainder of the staff must make do when adults are absent from their jobs.

Program Component	Appropriate Practice	Inappropriate Practice
Environment	The environment reflects the program's philosophy and goals. There is enough usable space so that children and youth are not crowded and the program's goals and objectives can be accomplished.	The environment is crowded, poorly equipped, messy or dirty, or generally uninviting to children and youth. There is not enough usable space to accommodate the program, or space is shared with multiple programs with different goals and objectives that limit the way the space can be used.
	Program staff have access to the space in sufficient time to prepare the environment for school-agers' arrival.	Space is available for set-up only as children and youth begin to arrive at the program. Staff are forced to contend with both physical space set-up and arriving children and youth.
	The environment is arranged to accommodate children and youth individually, in small groups, and in a large group and to facilitate a wide variety of activities.	The environment is conducive to only one type of activity, forcing children and youth to deal with a limited array of options or no options at all.
	Opportunities are available for children and youth to modify and personalize the environment.	Children and youth are not able to label storage bins with their names, display their creations, move furniture to create privacy, create signs for activity centers, put up posters of popular performing artists, or otherwise make the environment more reflective of themselves.
	Space is available for storing the materials and equipment needed to implement the program. Extra space is available for storing multistage projects and for displaying school-agers' work.	Storage space is so limited that neither children and youth nor staff are encouraged to plan multistage projects or prepare appropriate environments.
	A sufficient quantity of materials and equipment is provided for the number of children and youth enrolled. Materials are durable and in good repair. Extra materials are available for children or youth who make mistakes and wish to start over.	Available equipment and materials are limited. Games are incomplete; available materials are no longer functional or interesting to children and youth. Only one set of materials per program participant is allowed.

Program Component	Appropriate Practice	Inappropriate Practice
Environment (continued)	A system is in place for staff to secure necessary materials and supplies as needed to implement the program.	Programs are equipped at the beginning of the program year and not again until next year. Minimal or no resources are available for providing replacement of consumable materials or for acquisition of novel and new toys, games, and materials.
	Children and youth have opportunities to provide input into the acquisition of new materials and equipment.	The program is reequipped without seeking or considering program participants' input.
	The environment is arranged to provide private areas where children and youth can play or work alone or with a friend indoors and outdoors. Soft elements, such as rugs, cushions, bean bag chairs, and soft furniture, are included in the environment.	The environment contains only institutional furniture, such as tables, desks, and bleachers. Few or no accommodations are made for privacy or softness.
	Outdoor space is accessible to the program and is protected from access to streets and other dangers. When play areas are accessible to the public, clear boundaries are identified to children and youth and supervision of enrolled children and youth can be maintained.	Outdoor areas are shared with the public without special arrangements for access and use by the program. Staff cannot tell which children and youth are in the program and which are not.
Health and Safety	A procedure for accountability when a child or youth fails to arrive for the program is in placed and is followed.	Children and youth who do not arrive at the program are assumed to be absent, at home, or otherwise occupied. No attempt is made to learn their whereabouts.
	A system exists to ensure the safety of children and youth whose parents choose to allow them to leave the program on their own. The system includes written agreements between parents and the program and consistent sign-out procedures.	No system monitors departure of children and youth who have parents' permission to leave the program on their own.

Program Component	Appropriate Practice	Inappropriate Practice
Nutrition and Food Service	Snacks are nutritionally sound and are planned to meet each program participant's nutritional requirements as recommended by the Child Care Food Program of the U.S. Department of Agriculture.	Snacks consist of low-nutrition foods, such as potato chips, punch, cookies, or candy. Little or no effort is made to balance each program participant's nutritional requirements.
	The amount of food available to children and youth takes into consideration the length of time the child or youth is in the program and the amount of food needed by children and youth at different developmental stages.	Serving sizes are uniform. Extra snacks are not available for children and youth who need or want them.
	The timing of snacks takes into account school-agers' different eating schedules outside the program. Individual children and youth regulate the amount and timing of their own snacks.	All children and youth receive snacks at the same time, regardless of when they last ate or whether or not they are hungry at that time. Program participants are put in the position of either eating now or not getting any snack during the program day.
	Children and youth prepare and serve their own snacks as a routine part of the program.	Snacks are prepared and served by staff to prevent messes and spills.

**Examples of Program Planning and Assessment Tools
Based on *Developmentally Appropriate Practice***

Examples of Program Planning and Assessment Tools
Based on *Developmentally Appropriate Practice*

Developmentally Appropriate Practice in School-Age Child Care Programs was developed during a two-year process involving school-age child care practitioners across the country. It represents professionally endorsed guidelines for programs designed specifically for school-age children.

Developmentally Appropriate Practice should not be viewed simply as a reference document. Program planners, administrators, supervisors, and technical assistance providers will gain greater value from the publication by using it to create practical quality-improvement tools. By lifting and adapting pieces of the document, providers can develop a variety of tools tailored to their program's specific needs and current concerns.

Developmentally Appropriate Practice and tools derived from it can be used in many tasks, including:

- ► Program planning

- ► Policy and procedure development

- ► Staff training and development

- ► Program evaluation

- ► Grant application and proposal writing

- ► Approaches to policymakers

Following are a few examples of tools that can be created from *Developmentally Appropriate Practice.* None of these is intended to be used as is. Rather, school-age child care providers are encouraged to build from these examples to create resources relevant to their own programs, priorities, and concerns.

Example of *Developmentally Appropriate Practice* used in Program Planning for Parent Involvement

Practice

Appropriate: The program offers parents a variety of ways to be involved that provide all parents with real opportunities to participate. *(p.33)*

Inappropriate: Participation options are limited to parents coming to the program to meet with staff or to participate in activities. All participation options require attendance at the program's site during traditional work hours. *(p.33)*

Strategies for Implementing Appropriate Practice

Arrange field trips to parents' work sites.

Invite parents to share family history, cultural information, special skill, job experience, etc. Arrange for sharing via audio or video tape or in writing.

Encourage staff to make home visits when parent asks and/or situation indicates.

Solicit parent contributions to program newsletter.

Ask for parent input to program planning and evaluation.

Seek verbal or written feedback from parents on child's experience in program.

Practice

Appropriate: Communication with parents is open and fluid. Information on a program participant's accomplishments is shared with parents as often as are concerns about the child or youth. *(p.33)*

Inappropriate: Communication with parents occurs on a pre-set schedule, such as once a year, and addresses specific topics. Communication focuses on the school-ager's misbehavior or problems in the program. *(p.33)*

Strategies for Implementing Appropriate Practice

Parent bulletin board.

Parent newsletter.

Staff has informal conversation with parent each day at pick-up time.

Staff conversations with parent emphasize child's improvements, accomplishments.

Drop-in visits are encouraged.

Parent handbook is written in clear language.

Example of *Developmentally Appropriate Practice* used to establish Policy and Procedures regarding Guidance and Discipline

POLICY

THIS PROGRAM USES POSITIVE GUIDANCE AND DISCIPLINE TECHNIQUES TO HELP CHILDREN AND YOUTH ACHIEVE SELF-CONTROL AND DEVELOP THEIR CONSCIENCES. *(Principle 5, p.8)*

Procedures for dealing with inappropriate behavior

1. **Prevent troublesome behavior in the first place.** For example:

   Involve children and youth in establishing clear limits and rules. *(p.8)*

   Explain expectations for behavior. *(p.8)*

   Explain reasons and rationales for rules. *(p.8)*

   Provide duplicates of popular toys and materials, especially for younger children. *(p.8)*

   Adjust the size of the activity space in accordance with the amount of materials available for that activity. *(p.8)*

2. **When behavior that violates established rules begins to occur,** try:

   redirecting the child's or youth's attention *(p.8)*

   (for younger children) suggesting or (for older children and youth) asking for ideas about other activities that would be of interest *(p.8)*

3. **If unacceptable behavior persists, help the child or youth recognize and solve the problem.** For example:

   Talk with the child or youth privately and calmly. View the discussion as problem solving rather than discipline. *(p.28)*

   Ask the child or youth to verbalize the program's rule regarding the behavior. *(p.28)*

   Ask the child or youth to explain the reason for the rule. *(p.28)*

   Help the child or youth name several ways to solve the problem. *(p.8)*

   Help the child or youth understand how her/his actions might make others feel. (e.g., role-play, help label feelings). *(p.28)*

   Help child or youth identify possible or likely consequences if the behavior continues (e.g., "other kids won't want to play with me;" "I won't get to use the building blocks for a week"). *(p.28)*

4. **Understand that every infraction does not warrant attention.** *(p.28)*

5. **If conflict becomes physical, intervene immediately and use positive problem-solving methods outlined above.** *(p.29)*

Example of Staff Evaluation Form based on *Developmentally Appropriate Practice*

Appropriate Practice	Performance of Practice				Examples/Comments
	Seldom does this; re-sists chang-ing approach when prompted.	Sometimes does this; usually responds when prompted.	Frequently does this; responds quickly when prompted.	Does this routinely; is staff member's typical approach.	
Staff member evidences understanding of the role that staff play in school-agers' lives.					
Interacts frequently with children and youth individually and in small groups as they work and play. *(p.23)*	1	2	3	4	
Seeks meaningful conversations with school-agers and spends more time listening to what they have to say than talking. *(p.23)*	1	2	3	4	
Points out events that may be missed, offers suggestions, and provides encouragement and recognition for effort as well as recognition for accomplishment. *(p.24)*	1	2	3	4	
Treats children and youth of both sexes and all races, religions, family backgrounds, and cultures equally with respect and consideration. Encourages the same behavior in school-agers. *(p.24)*	1	2	3	4	
Stays in physical or line-of-sight proximity to children and youth. *(p.25)*	1	2	3	4	
Positions self strategically and is aware of the activities of the entire group even when dealing with a part of it. *(p.25)*	1	2	3	4	
Plans ahead to prevent problem situations from occurring. Uses his/her knowledge of school-agers' skills and abilities to anticipate what they need and what they need to do. *(p.25)*	1	2	3	4	

Appropriate Practice	Performance of Practice				Examples/Comments
	Seldom does this; resists changing approach when prompted.	Sometimes does this; usually responds when prompted.	Frequently does this; responds quickly when prompted.	Does this routinely; is staff member's typical approach.	
Recognizes the need of school-age children and youth for autonomy and independence. (p.25)	1	2	3	4	
Sees her/his primary role as one of facilitation rather than direction. (p.3)	1	2	3	4	
Assists school-agers with developing their own skills and abilities by setting the context, suggesting activities and experiences, providing guidance, and serving as a resource. (p.3)	1	2	3	4	
Prepares the environment and provides suggestions for possible activities from which children in the early childhood years may choose. (p.3)	1	2	3	4	
Serves as a motivator for participation in activities by children in the early childhood stage through actions and presence. (p.3)	1	2	3	4	
Involves school-agers in middle childhood in setting the stage for activities (e.g., distributing materials, arranging props, and getting out equipment). (p.3)	1	2	3	4	
Shares responsibilities with early adolescents for initiating and arranging activities. Participates with these school-agers as equals. (p.3)	1	2	3	4	
Staff member uses positive guidance and discipline techniques to help children and youth achieve self-control and develop their consciences.					
Involves children and youth in establishing clear limits and rules. (p.8)	1	2	3	4	
Explains reasons and rationales for rules as well as expectations for behavior. (p.8)	1	2	3	4	
Helps children and youth evaluate different approaches to problem solving. (p.8)	1	2	3	4	

Example of *Developmentally Appropriate Practice* in a Checklist for Assessing the Environment

Principle 6: Environments in developmentally appropriate school-age child care programs are arranged to accommodate children and youth individually, in small groups, and in large groups, and to facilitate a wide variety of activities and experiences. *(pp.10, 30-31)*

Space is arranged so children and youth can work individually. *(p.10)*	Yes	No
Space is arranged so children and youth can work in small groups. *(p.10)*	Yes	No
Space is arranged so children and youth can work in a large group. *(p.10)*	Yes	No
There are private spaces where children and youth can be alone and get away from the larger group. *(p.10)*	Yes	No
The environment has soft elements such as pillows, carpets, bean bag chairs, and gymnastics mats. *(p.10)*	Yes	No
There is enough usable space so that children and youth are not crowded. *(p.35)*	Yes	No
There is a sufficient variety of materials to meet children's and youth's interests. *(p.10)*	Yes	No
A sufficient quantity of materials and equipment is provided for the number of children and youth enrolled. Extra materials are available for children or youth who wish to start over. *(p.35)*	Yes	No
Materials are durable and in good repair. *(p.35)*	Yes	No
Materials are readily accessible to children and youth. *(p.10)*	Yes	No
Children and youth have many opportunities to personalize the environment with products of their work and play. *(p.10)*	Yes	No
(If the space is used for other types of activities when the program is not in session:) Creative storage systems facilitate quick conversion of the space into a school-age child care environment and back. *(p.10)*	Yes	No
Extra space is available for storing multi-stage projects. *(p.35)*	Yes	No
Staff involve children and youth in setting up and taking down the toys, materials, and activity areas, making this type of activity a component of the program. *(p.10)*	Yes	No

Examples of *Developmentally Appropriate Practice* on Anchored Rating Scales for Assessing Staff Interactions

On each scale, circle the number that shows how closely your program resembles the description on the left or on the right.

Staff interact predominantly with large groups. *(p.23)*	-2 -1 0 1 2	Staff interact frequently with children and youth individually and in small groups as they work and play.
Staff display differential treatment of children and youth based on gender or background. *(p.24)*	-2 -1 0 1 2	Staff treat children and youth of both genders and all races, religions, family backgrounds, and cultures equally with respect, attention, and consideration.
Staff determine the pace and sequence of the day and what activities will be available to whom. *(p.26)*	-2 -1 0 1 2	Children and youth play a central role in determining the activities and experiences in which they participate; choice predominates.
Staff seldom include children and youth in problem solution. Consequences are primarily adult determined. *(p.28)*	-2 -1 0 1 2	Logical and natural consequences and negotiated outcomes are used to resolve conflicts and problems.
Staff talk about parents in a negative way to other staff members and in front of children and youth. When problems arise, staff assume the problems arise from poor parenting. *(p.33)*	-2 -1 0 1 2	Staff speak respectfully of parents and believe parents act in their school-ager's best interest.
Large numbers of children and youth have few staff for guidance and support. *(p.34)*	-2 -1 0 1 2	Group size and the ratio of staff to children and youth are limited to insure active involvement of staff and support for children and youth.

References

References

Asher, S.R., & Coil, J. D. (1990). *Peer rejection in childhood.* New York: Cambridge University Press.

Asher, S.R., Renshaw, P., & Hymel, S. (1982). Peer relations and development of social skills. In S. Moore & C. Cooper (Eds.), *The young child: Reviews of research* (Vol. 3). Washington, DC: National Association for the Education of Young Children.

Bender, J., Schuyler-Haas Elder, B., & Flatter, C.H. (1984). *Half a childhood.* Nashville, TN: School Age NOTES.

Bergstrom, J.M. (1990). *School's out.* Berkley, CA: Ten Speed Press.

Bredekamp, S. (Ed.). (1987). *Developmentally appropriate practice in early childhood programs serving children from birth to age 8.* Washington, DC: National Association for the Education of Young Children.

Collins, W.A. (1984). *Development during middle childhood: The years from six to twelve.* Washington, DC: National Academy Press.

Coopersmith, S. (1967). *The antecedents of self-esteem.* San Francisco, CA: Freeman.

Curry, N.E., & Johnson, C.N. (1990). *Beyond self-esteem: Developing a genuine sense of human value.* Washington, DC: National Association for the Education of Young Children.

Erickson, E. (1963). *Childhood and society.* New York, NY: Norton.

Gecas, V. (1982). The self-concept. *Annual Review of Sociology, 8,* 1-33.

Harter, S. (1986). Processes underlying the construction, maintenance, and enhancement of the self-concept in children. In J. Suls & G. Greenwald (Eds.), *Psychological perspectives of the self* (Vol. 3). Hillsdale, NJ: Earlbaum.

Katz, L.G., Evangelou, D., & Hartman, J.A. (1990). *The case for mixed-age grouping in early education.* Washington, DC: National Association for the Education of Young Children.

Kohlberg, L. (1976). Moral stages and moralization: The cognitive developmental approach. In T. Lickona (Ed.), *Moral development and behavior.* New York, NY: Holt, Rinehart and Winston.

Lickona, T. (1983). *Raising good children.* New York, NY: Bantam.

Maccoby, E.E. (1980). *Social development.* New York, NY: Harcourt, Brace, Jovanovich.

Marion, M. (1987). *Guidance of young children.* Columbus, OH: Merrill.

Oden, S., & Asher, S.R. (1977). Coaching children in social skills for friendship making. *Child Development, 48,* 495-506.

Piaget, J. (1952). *The child's conception of number.* London: Routledge & Kegan Paul.

Selman, R.L. (1981). The child as a friendship philosopher. In S. Asher & J. Gottman (Eds.), *The development of children's friendships.* Cambridge, MA: Cambridge University Press.

Shaffer, D.R. (1979). *Social and personality development.* Belmont, CA: Wadsworth.

Stright, A.L., & French, D.C. (1988). Leadership in mixed-age children's groups. *International Journal of Behavioral Development, 11,* 507-515.

Vygotsky, L.S. (1978). *Mind in society: The development of higher psychological processes* (M. Cole, V. John-Steiner, S. Scribner, & E. Souberman, Eds. and trans.). Cambridge, MA: Harvard University Press.

Webster, M., & Sobieszek, B. (1974). *Sources of self-evaluation: A formal theory of significant others and social influences.* New York, NY: John Wiley.

Wylie, R. (1979). *The self-concept* (Vol. 2, Rev. ed.). Lincoln, NE: University of Nebraska Press.

Appendices

Appendix 1

Project Home Safe
Developmentally Appropriate Practice Steering Committee

Kay M. Albrecht, Committee Chair
Senior Partner
Child Care Management Associates
P.O. Box 820687
Houston, TX 77282-0687
713/493-2262

Sue Bredekamp
Director of Professional Development
National Association for the Education of
  Young Children
1834 Connecticut Avenue, NW
Washington, DC 20009
202/232-8777

Mick Coleman
Human Development Specialist
Assistant Professor of Child and Family
  Development
Georgia Cooperative Extension Service
Home Economics, Hoke-Smith Annex
University of Georgia
Athens, GA 30602
706/542-4882

Richard T. Scofield, Editor
School-Age NOTES
P.O. Box 120674
Nashville, TN 37212
615/242-8464

Christine M. Todd
Assistant Professor and Child Development
  Specialist
Cooperative Extension Service
University of Illinois
543 Bevier Hall
Urbana, IL 61801
217/244-1290

Participants in Working Forum on School-Age Child Care Standards

Kay M. Albrecht, Forum Facilitator
Senior Partner
Child Care Management Associates
P.O. Box 820687
Houston, TX 77282-0687
713/493-2262

Betsy Arns, Instructor
School-Age Child Care
P.O. Box 5012
Huntington Beach, CA 92615-5012
714/556-3357

Tracey Ballas
Education & Training Associate
Wellesley College School-Age Child Care
  Project
1742 Norwood Boulevard
Zanesville, OH 43701
614/453-7743

Joan Bergstrom, Professor
Wheelock College
303 Marsh Street
Belmont, MA 02178
617/734-5200

Cheryl Camp
Community Recreation Specialist
Naval Military Personnel Command (N-651C)
Washington, DC 20370
703/746-6478

Sheryl L. Cohn, Educational Psychologist
School Age Child Care Consultant
136 Concord Street
New Milford, NJ 07646
201/385-9802

Mick Coleman
Human Development Specialist
Assistant Professor of Child and Family
 Development
Georgia Cooperative Extension Service
Home Economics, Hoke-Smith Annex
University of Georgia
Athens, GA 30602
404/542-8881

Susan Conklin, Head
Community Recreation
Naval Military Personnel Command (N-651C)
Washington, DC 20370
703/746-6478

Nick Craft
Legal/Legislative Chairman
Georgia Child Care Association
Learning Tree of America
605 Rome Street
Carrollton, GA 30117
404/834-2353

Diane E. Curl, President
Board of Directors
California School Age Consortium
280 Dolores Street
San Francisco, CA 94103
415/550-1536

Laurie Dopkins, Chair
Public Policy Committee
School-Age Child Care Council
470 Chelsea Circle
Atlanta, GA 30307
404/378-2279

Barbara Dubovich
Camp Fire, Alaska Council
3745 Community Park Drive, #104
Anchorage, AK 99508
907/279-3551

Colleen Dyrud, Coordinator
School Age Child Care Project
Oregon Department of Education
700 Pringle Parkway, SE
Salem, OR 97310
503/378-5585

Barbara Fierro, Executive Director
Big Brothers and Big Sisters of the Black
 Hills
924 Quincy Street
Rapid City, SD 57702
605/343-1488

Ruth L. Fitzpatrick, Director
School-Age Child Care
Kentucky Department of Education
1730 Capital Plaza Tower
Frankfort, KY 40601
502/564-6117

Ellen Gannett, Education and Training
 Coordinator
School-Age Child Care Project
Wellesley College Center for
 Research on Women
Wellesley, MA 02181
617/283-2456

Emerson M. Goodwin, Manager
Program Youth Development
National 4-H Council
7100 Connecticut Avenue
Chevy Chase, MD 20815
301/961-2897

Karen Haas-Foletta, Director
West Portal C.A.R.E.
5 Lenox Way
San Francisco, CA 94127
415/753-1113

Kate Hacker
Special Projects for Children
17 Brookmont Circle
San Anselmo, CA 94960
415/456-4699

Suzanne Hancock
Youth Program Leader
601 Rosery Road, E., #1151
Largo, FL 34640-3816
407/539-6269

Barbara A. Harvey, Field Coordinator
School District of Philadelphia
First Methodist Get Set Day Care Center
Germantown Avenue & High Street
Philadelphia, PA 19144
215/843-4038

Deborah Kenyon, Unit Director
Joseph B. Whitehead Boys Club
1900 Lakewood Avenue, SE
Atlanta, GA 30315
404/627-4617

Sally A. Koblinsky, Professor
Family and Community Development
College of Human Ecology
Marie Mount Hall, Room 1204
University of Maryland
College Park, MD 20742
301/405-4009

Joyce Lang, Assistant Director for Child
   Care Services
Community Services for Children, Inc.
431 East Locust Street
Bethlehem, PA 18018
215/691-1819

Leah M. Lefstein, Deputy Director
Indiana Youth Institute
333 N. Alabama, Suite 200
Indianapolis, IN 46204
317/634-4222

Mary Elizabeth Leggat
Regional Supervisor
School-Age Child Care Program
Fairfax County Office for Children
3701 Pender Drive
Fairfax, VA 22030
703/938-4370

M.-A. Lucas, Chief
Army Child Development Services
HQDA (CFSC-FSC)
Hoffman Building I, Room 1408
Alexandria, VA 22331-0521
703/325-0710

Tom Massey, Associate Director
Program Services
YMCA of the USA
101 North Wacker Drive
Chicago, IL 60606
312/269-0516

Ruth T. Matthews
Camp Fire SACC
P.O. Box 985
Stowe, VT 05662
802/828-8771

Ina Lynn McClain
State 4-H Youth Development Specialist
212 Whitten Hall
University of Missouri
Columbia, MO 65211
314/882-4319

Frankie McMurrey
Clayton Child Care, Inc.
2747 8th Avenue
Ft. Worth, TX 76110
817/926-9381

Victoria B. Moss, Program Manager
Supplemental Programs & Services
Army Child Development Services
HQDA (CFSC-FSC)
Hoffman Building I, Room 1408
Alexandria, VA 22331-0521
703/325-0710

Jan Ockunzzi, Project Director
Florida School-Age Child Care Clearinghouse
LATCHKEY Services for Children, Inc.
4910-D Creekside Drive
Clearwater, FL 34620
813/573-1060

Chris Payne, Research Associate
Department of Child and Family Research
Western Carolina Center
300 Enola Road
Morganton, NC 28655
704/433-2618

Stephen W. Pratt, Chief
Youth Services
U.S. Army Community & Family Support
   Center
Room 1425
(CFSC-FSY-Y) Hoffman Building
2461 Eisenhower Avenue
Alexandria, VA 22331-0521
703/325-8377

Flo Reinmuth
Action for Children
92 Jefferson Avenue
Columbus, OH 43215
614/837-2016
614/846-0050

Lydia Roberts
Child Care Program Specialist
Cabinet for Human Resources
Department for Social Services
275 East Main Street, Sixth Floor West
Frankfort, KY 40621
502/564-2136

Leslie Roesler, Project Director
Day Care Association of Montgomery
   County, Inc.
Southeastern Pennsylvania School Age Child
   Care Project
601 Knight Road
Ambler, PA 19002
215/643-3841

Karen Miller Rush
Child Care Director
Goshen Area Camp Fire H.E.L.P. Program
Box 506
Goshen, IN 46526
219/533-4590

Peter Scales, Deputy Director
Center for Early Adolescence
University of North Carolina at Chapel Hill
Carr Mill Mall, Suite 211
Carrboro, NC 27510
919/966-1148

Joy A. Schrage, Manager
Appliance Information Service
Whirlpool Corporation
2000 M-63 North
Benton Harbor, MI 49022
616/923-3164

Richard T. Scofield, Editor
School-Age NOTES
P.O. Box 120674
Nashville, TN 37212
615/242-8464

Michelle Seligson, Director
School-Age Child Care Project
Wellesley College Center for Research on
   Women
Wellesley, MA 02181
617/283-2546

Deborah Shepherd, Coordinator
Troy School District
Adult and Community Education
201 West Square Lake Road
Troy, MI 48098
313/879-7582

Mary M. Shiffer
107 S. Spring Street
Bellefonte, PA 16823
814/353-0216

Roxanne Spillett, Assistant National Director
Program Services
Boys & Girls Clubs of America
771 First Avenue
New York, NY 10017
212/351-5906

Christine M. Todd
Assistant Professor and Child Development
   Specialist
Cooperative Extension Service
University of Illinois
543 Bevier Hall
Urbana, IL 61801
217/244-1290

Judy Tough, School Age Child Care
   Consultant
Action for Children
92 Jefferson
Columbus, OH 43215
614/224-0222
614/486-0075

Gladys Gary Vaughn, Director
Research and Public Policy
American Home Economics Association
1555 King Street
Alexandria, VA 22314
703/706-4600

Lynn L. White, Executive Director
Georgia Child Care Association
1029 Railroad Street, NW
Conyers, GA 30207
404/483-2408

Kay Anne Wilbourn, Executive Assistant
Office of Instruction
Kentucky Department of Education
1723 Capitol Plaza Tower
Frankfort, KY 40601
502/564-3010

Dellie Woodring, Executive Director
Kentfield After School Center
22 Cypress Avenue
Kentfield, CA 94904
415/453-4100

Appendix 2

Project Home Safe Description

Project Home Safe, a program of the American Home Economics Association funded in part by a grant from Whirlpool Foundation, promotes safe and appropriate out-of-school arrangements for school-age children. The Project provides materials, training, and other resources to help parents and communities consider a range of child care options and select the best solutions for their needs. Project Home Safe has four components.

*   *   *   *   *

National School-Age Child Care Resource Center. Project Home Safe's resource center distributes materials on self-care and school-age child care to parents, educators, youth leaders, program developers, employers, and others concerned with the problem of out-of-school care for school-agers. The center can be called toll free at 800/252-SAFE. Resources include:

- ▸ brochures for parents on assessing readiness and preparing for self-care and on finding high-quality school-age child care programs that meet individual child's needs;

- ▸ tips for parents with children in self-care on home and personal safety; after-school activities; dealing with boredom, loneliness, and fear; healthful snacks; and self-care books for parents and children;

- ▸ bibliographies on children's safety materials, activities for children at home, family-oriented self-care guides, libraries and latchkey children, telephone helplines for children, self-care videos, and research on self-care;

- ▸ guidelines for professionals on quality school-age child care programming;

- ▸ bibliographies on school-age child care development and operation, activities and curricula, and staff training; school-, church-, and family day care-based programs; intergenerational programs; serving children with special needs; child care advocacy; employers and child care; and audiovisual resources; and

- ▸ information on ways volunteers can help improve child care options for school-age children and their families.

*   *   *   *   *

Community Training and Involvement. The Project's community training program, *Beyond the Latchkey: Expanding Community Options for School-Age Care*, prepares community leaders and volunteers to address local latchkey and school-age child care issues. During the action-oriented training, participants explore a range of options for providing care for school-agers.

After training, often working with local organizations, participants develop and implement initiatives to meet the child care needs of school-agers and their parents. Participants design projects based on their own interests, their professional roles, and the needs and resources of their communities.

In the program's first five years, community-based trainers trained more than 650 youth leaders, teachers, child care advocates, and other concerned individuals in 23 states. Those participants went on to reach over half a million children and adults by giving workshops on self-care for children and parents, creating supportive services for children at home alone, developing and improving the quality of school-age child care programs, and advocating for public and private sector policies responsive to families' child care responsibilities.

Initially, training programs were hosted by state home economics associations. Based on their success, the program has expanded to additional professions, interest groups, and communities. National service and advocacy organizations are working in partnership with the Project to disseminate *Beyond the Latchkey* through their local and regional networks.

*   *   *   *   *

Research on Self-Care. High-quality research on latchkey children is limited. Project Home Safe awarded two grants for research on topics related to children in self-care. A $40,000 professional grant has supported a study of the predictors and consequences of the amount of time children spend in self-care. A $10,000 graduate student grant has supported a study of sibling caretakers' perceptions of their role. Findings from both studies can improve the quality of society's response to the problem of children at home alone.

*   *   *   *   *

School-Age Child Care Quality Initiative. Until 1991, there were no nationally recognized standards for child care programs designed specifically for school-age children. Project Home Safe sponsored an initiative to develop two resources for quality school-age child care programming.

▶ *Developmentally Appropriate Practice in School-Age Child Care Programs* provides guidelines for programming tailored to the characteristics and needs of school-age children. It presents principles of developmentally appropriate programming illustrated with specific practices--both appropriate and inappropriate--related to various program components.

▶ *Quality Criteria for School-Age Child Care Programs* specifies indicators of high quality in programs for school-agers. The criteria address key program components such as staffing, interactions with children and youth, activities and experiences, the environment, and parent involvement.

School-age child care practitioners and child development specialists across the country helped develop and review these publications. Program planners and providers are using them to assess, expand, and improve programming for school-agers, train and orient staff, and inform parents and policy makers about developmental issues and program quality. The resources also are helping define accreditation and licensing requirements for school-age child care programs, and are valuable resources for college child development and program planning courses.

Appendix 3

Project Home Safe National Advisory Committee

Kay M. Albrecht, Ph.D.
Senior Partner
Innovations in Early Childhood Education
(formerly Child Care Management
    Associates)
Houston, Texas

Mick Coleman, Ph.D.
Associate Professor of Child and Family
    Development
College of Family and Consumer Science
Athens, Georgia

Jean D. Dickerscheid, Ph.D., C.H.E.
Associate Dean, The Graduate School
The Ohio State University
Columbus, Ohio

Carolyn S. Dorrell, M.Ed.
Director of Community Educational Services
ETV Network
Columbia, South Carolina

Cynthia E. Johnson, Ph.D., C.H.E.
Human Development Specialist
Agricultural Extension Service
North Carolina State University
Raleigh, North Carolina

Sally A. Koblinsky, Ph.D.
Professor
Family and Community Development
College of Human Ecology
University of Maryland
College Park, Maryland

Rebecca P. Lovingood, Ph.D., C.H.E.
Professor
College of Human Resources
Virginia Polytechnic Institute and State
    University
Blacksburg, Virginia

The Honorable Donald W. Riegle, Jr.
United States Senator, Michigan
Washington, DC

Joy A. Schrage, M.S., C.H.E.
Consultant
Consumer Communications Services, Inc.
Berrien Center, Michigan

Christine M. Todd, Ph.D.
Child Development Specialist
School of Human Development and Family
    Studies
University of Illinois
Urbana, Illinois

Ex-officio Members

Stephen E. Upton
President
Whirlpool Foundation
Benton Harbor, Michigan

Gladys Gary Vaughn, Ph.D., C.H.E.
Project Creator and Monitor
Acting Director of Development
American Home Economics Association
    Foundation
Alexandria, Virginia

Mary Jane Kolar, CAE
Executive Director
American Home Economics Association
Alexandria, Virginia

Project Staff

Margaret C. Plantz, Ph.D.
Project Director

Ann C. Walsh
Administrative Assistant

Former Staff

Sally A. Koblinsky, Ph.D.
Project Director, 1987-88

Loretta B. Lynch
Program Associate, 1987-88

Maren L. Proulx
Program Associate, 1988-90

Susan Marcus Bushnell
Field Services Coordinator, 1991-92